Top Gear

Race to the North Pole

This is **brilliant!**

BBC Children's Books
Published by the Penguin Group
Penguin Books Ltd, 80 Strand, London WC2R 0RL, England
Penguin Group (Australia) Ltd, 250 Camberwell Road,
Camberwell, Victoria 3124, Australia (a division of Pearson
Australia Group Pty Ltd)
Canada, India, New Zealand, South Africa

Published by BBC Children's Books, 2009
Text and design © Children's Character Books, 2009
This edition produced for The Book People Ltd, Hall Wood
Avenue, Haydock, St Helens, WA11 9UL

10 9 8 7 6 5 4 3 2 1

Written by Jonathan Empson

ISBN: 978-1-40590-657-9

Printed in China

He's a **plucky** Brit
and like all plucky
Brits, he's going to
come **second.**

Contents

You're not even doing this **intelligently.**

I shall be travelling using **traditional** methods.

> No-one has **ever** tried to drive to the North Pole.

Introduction

Welcome to Top Gear's most ambitious race yet: to the North Pole. Normally, getting to the Pole involves months of planning, physical training and shouting "Mush!" to a team of huskies. But Jeremy Clarkson has had a better idea: he's going to bung some fat tyres on a 4x4 and simply drive there – a total of 400 miles over Arctic ice, starting from Canada's most northern town, Resolute.

In the passenger seat will be James May. His job: to keep tabs on how cold it is and to navigate – luckily, this just involves making sure the compass needle is always pointing to 'N'.

I'm only here because the producer said I **had** to be. I **don't** like snow. I **hate** being cold. I **hate** outdoor pursuits. I **can't stand** this stupid clothing that makes this rustling noise when you move.

LONDON - 6831 - M

SEOUL 6680

Richard Hammond, meanwhile, will be trying to beat them to the Pole the old-fashioned way, aboard a sledge behind a team of huskies. He'll be trying not to get old-fashioned frostbite or be eaten by an old-fashioned polar bear.

Yes, the Arctic is jam-packed with danger, and has a worrying lack of ambulances and hospitals. Even worse, there are no hotels en route, so the boys will have to camp. Worse still, they'll be trying to sleep in broad daylight: up here, the sun never sets in summer.

So it's not a matter of who will win this race: will anybody even survive?

Let's go to the Pole!

The Car

TY07 HLX

> You will be the **first** person **ever** to go to the North Pole who **didn't** want to be there!

> I **hate** your stupid truck.

For this race, Jeremy and James will be placing their trust in a highly modified Toyota Hilux 4x4 from Iceland.

Wheels

The wheelarches are flared by 30cm to house the giant 38in snow tyres. These are handmade and cost £2500 each. They contain metal studs for traction (rather than fashion) and their huge size helps spread the weight. Useful when you're driving across thin sea ice.

Differentials

These are the devices that distribute the engine's power to the wheels. On this Hilux, they're lockable (to stop wheelspin) and modified for the icy conditions.

Shotgun

Polar bears are a threatened species. This gun will help Jeremy and James threaten them even more. Hopefully they won't use it on each other.

Engine

A modified 164hp 3-litre diesel with a heater for the fuel and one for the coolant – in these temperatures, the coolant gets too cool when the engine's switched off.

Gadgets

It's got a GPS marine navigation system, a satellite phone, VHF two-way radio, an air compressor (for inflating the tyres), cameras (so you can watch Jeremy and James arguing) and an inverter to give 220V mains power.

Winch

For pulling themselves out of trouble. Of course, in the Arctic the real challenge is finding something to attach it to.

VRROOOMM

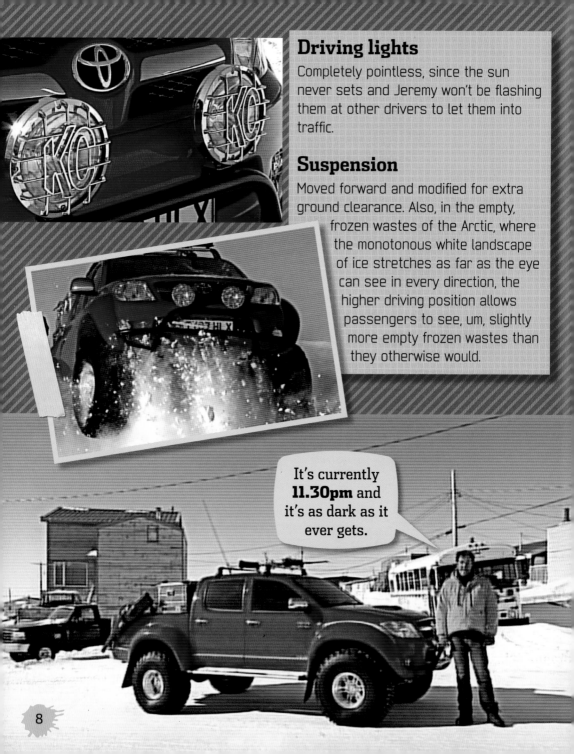

Driving lights

Completely pointless, since the sun never sets and Jeremy won't be flashing them at other drivers to let them into traffic.

Suspension

Moved forward and modified for extra ground clearance. Also, in the empty, frozen wastes of the Arctic, where the monotonous white landscape of ice stretches as far as the eye can see in every direction, the higher driving position allows passengers to see, um, slightly more empty frozen wastes than they otherwise would.

It's currently **11.30pm** and it's as dark as it ever gets.

Kit

Besides the spare tyre (in case they manage to run over the only nail in the Arctic), the load bay contains boxes full of useful gear including shovels, jacks, crowbars, toolkits, a towing strap, first aid equipment and a chainsaw – obviously for sawing through ice rather than trees.

Skid plates

These 5mm-thick aluminium plates are designed to protect the engine and transmission when driving over very rough ground. They'll be needed.

Extra fuel tank

This isn't an economy run, and petrol stations are thin on the ground out here. The 100-litre extra tank and the 80-litre standard one are filled with a freeze-resistant mix of diesel and avgas (the stuff that planes run on).

Other people

Look, somebody had to film Jeremy and James doing their thing. But the support crew, travelling in two additional vehicles, includes Icelandic guides and mechanics, a doctor and a Special Forces expert.

Team Dog

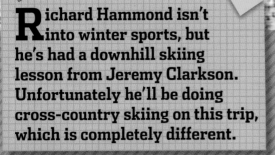

Richard Hammond isn't into winter sports, but he's had a downhill skiing lesson from Jeremy Clarkson. Unfortunately he'll be doing cross-country skiing on this trip, which is completely different.

Luckily his guide Matty McNair is an expert. She's skied to both the North Pole (the real one) and the South Pole. On one trip to the South Pole, she even took her kids along, so Richard should be no problem.

For this outing they'll mainly be on a sledge towed by 10 huskies: these dogs love the cold, and love to run.

A film crew will be travelling alongside on snowmobiles, to capture the moment when Richard conquers the top of the planet. Or the moment when he gets devoured by huskies who've mistaken him for a dog biscuit.

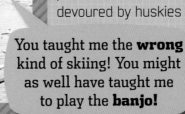

You taught me the **wrong** kind of skiing! You might as well have taught me to play the **banjo!**

Training

"**W**e're not what you'd call polar explorers," says Jeremy Clarkson. And that's not what you'd call an understatement – they have no idea what they're getting into.

Therefore, before being sent to Canada, the three Top Gear contenders are sent to the Austrian Alps for cold-weather training. A crack team of professionals guides them through essential survival information, such as...

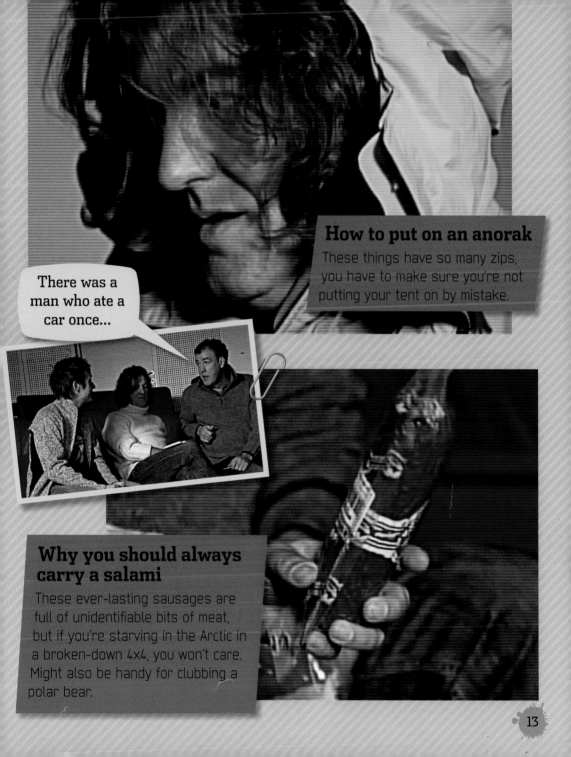

There was a man who ate a car once...

How to put on an anorak

These things have so many zips, you have to make sure you're not putting your tent on by mistake.

Why you should always carry a salami

These ever-lasting sausages are full of unidentifiable bits of meat, but if you're starving in the Arctic in a broken-down 4x4, you won't care. Might also be handy for clubbing a polar bear.

How to do a 'number two'

Polar bears, you see, like to creep up on you while you've got your trousers round your ankles.

That's not **exactly** sporting of them, is it?

You've got to be **quick.** Take your gun with you, and put your bog roll on your gun, and take a shovel.

CENSORED

The effect of frostbite on your dangly bits

You really don't want to know. Another reason to be quick when going to the loo.

ARRRGGH!

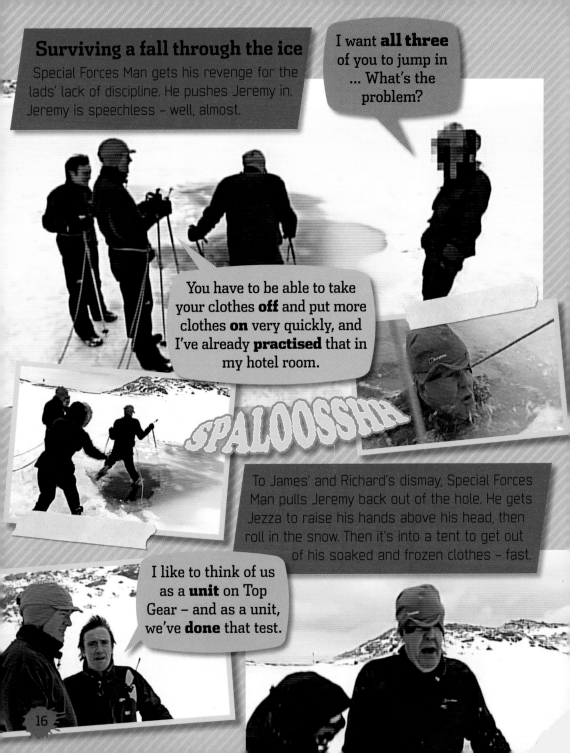

Surviving a fall through the ice

Special Forces Man gets his revenge for the lads' lack of discipline. He pushes Jeremy in. Jeremy is speechless – well, almost.

I want **all three** of you to jump in ... What's the problem?

You have to be able to take your clothes **off** and put more clothes **on** very quickly, and I've already **practised** that in my hotel room.

SPALOOSSHH

To James' and Richard's dismay, Special Forces Man pulls Jeremy back out of the hole. He gets Jezza to raise his hands above his head, then roll in the snow. Then it's into a tent to get out of his soaked and frozen clothes – fast.

I like to think of us as a **unit** on Top Gear – and as a unit, we've **done** that test.

You lot are apparently **ignorant.**

The hatred is **very** real.

How to take it seriously

Time for a good talking-to from legendary Arctic explorer Sir Ranulph Fiennes.

Sir Ranulph warns them they will all start hating each other because of the extreme cold.

But frostbite is the real danger. After getting his hand wet on one polar expedition, Sir R suffered such bad frostbite that he had to saw off the ends of his own fingers.

James asks about their chances of survival if the car falls through the ice. Sir R thinks they might live a few hours, "but in those circumstances I think I'd prefer to go quickly".

That was a three-minute mistake.

Race Preparation

I've just been **weed** on. Do they **have** to wee on me?

The Race Begins – Day 1

Race day is clear and sunny – which actually doesn't suit the huskies, who like it cold. Apparently it doesn't suit James either.

And they're off! And they stop! Well, Jeremy and James do because James has forgotten his gloves.

Richard and Matty take an early lead, but Jeremy and James soon blast past.

I can't believe it: I'm going to the Pole!

Look at that awful expanse of misery.

Not yet.

Are you cold? Are we falling through the ice?

Well cheer up.

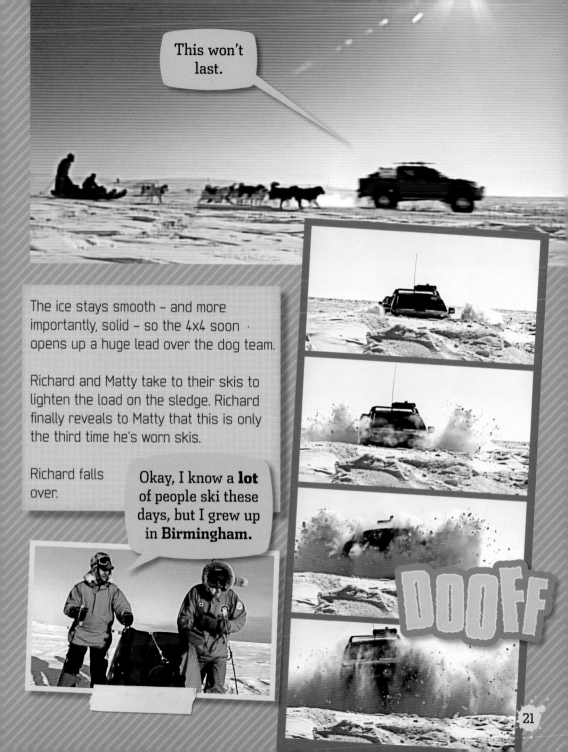

This won't last.

The ice stays smooth – and more importantly, solid – so the 4x4 soon opens up a huge lead over the dog team.

Richard and Matty take to their skis to lighten the load on the sledge. Richard finally reveals to Matty that this is only the third time he's worn skis.

Richard falls over.

Okay, I know a **lot** of people ski these days, but I grew up in **Birmingham**.

DOOFF

I think we could forge a career as the world's **worst** explorers.

It takes Jeremy and James three minutes to cover three miles. Jeremy is confident that they will reach the Pole in no time.

He tries to motivate his less than enthusiastic teammate.

At the end of Day 1, Richard is crippled after 10 hours on the go. Aiming to cover 50-60 miles, they've in fact only done 36. The sea ice contains salt, which makes it very grippy on the sledge's runners.

Like Richard, Jeremy and James have to camp. They can't just sleep in the car in case it falls through the ice. Jeremy would rather take the risk.

I'm **broken.**

Everything's **c*@p!**

23

Day 2

Oh, not on the ropes!

Richard's balaclava has frozen to his face overnight. His sleeping bag is covered in frost, too.

Things are more civilised in the car camp. Jeremy has fitted a 'bumper dumper' toilet seat to the towbar to make things more comfortable. James stands guard nearby, secretly hoping a bear will sneak up and devour Jeremy anyway.

Richard and Matty set off, following ten dogs who are all taking their morning toilet break.

I thought he could **guide** us in our hour of need, if we ever **have** one.

Jeremy and James, meanwhile, are stuffing their faces with chocolate bars. Polar explorers need to keep up their energy levels.

James discovers the Jesus doll Jeremy has decided to bring along.

Richard thinks he's starting to get the hang of skiing. Then Matty tells him he has to learn to pee on the move.

Richard falls over again.

I'm not on... **Matty!**

VARROOOMMM

Jeremy and James reach Bathurst Island, which is actually made of real land instead of frozen water. They extend their lead over Team Dog.

Richard stops to examine the remains of a seal at an aglu – a seal's breathing hole in the ice. Polar bears sometimes lie in wait for a seal to surface, then grab it.

Jeremy and James get bogged down in deep snow. But their Icelandic guides advise them just to let almost all the air out of the tyres. The flat tyres have a bigger 'footprint' and this helps get them unstuck.

Maybe it was full. **Hope** it still is.

TY07 HLX

RRRAAAAARRRRR

How **monstrous** is this?

It's not normal.

Back on firm snow, they pump the tyres back up using the on-board air compressor. Easy!

But all too soon it's time to camp again. Not so easy.

Richard and Matty have made good progress but they're still 50 miles behind. He and Matty devise a plan: grab a quick three-hour nap, then press on.

We're going to run at **night**, it's cooler for the dogs ... and they can run **faster** and **harder.**

27

Day 3

Richard and Matty rouse the dogs. It's -35°C. Nice weather for huskies.

Then they spot a polar bear! They have to watch which way it's heading – and if it seems peckish.

Over at the car camp, Jeremy sets off too – even though James hasn't quite finished, um...

Clarkson! I know it's you, you insufferable oaf!

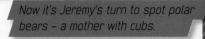

Now it's Jeremy's turn to spot polar bears – a mother with cubs.

Swwweeeet! It's got babies!

Perhaps the bears have caught a whiff of James' tin of Spam.

Of all the things you could have brought...

Richard, unsure whether it's day or night now, tries to get some sleep.

Jeremy and James make it to the other side of the island. They're so far ahead, Jeremy decides to try a bit of waterskiing – with real skis, on frozen water.

I'm confused. My body clock's broken.

TY07 HLX

Disaster! On James' first go behind the wheel, he crashes the Hilux into deep snow, and it's sinking into what looks like… sea water.

Luckily the Icelandic guides are on hand to drag the 4x4 out using a snatch strap – a big stretchy rope.

But it's a warning to the dangers of driving back on the frozen ocean. Tidal movement weakens the ice where the sea meets the land, so they should avoid driving near the shores. Trouble is, they're driving down a narrow fjord, less than a mile wide.

The ice is cracked and dangerously thin, but there's no alternative route because they're surrounded by cliffs – they must either press on or give up and turn back.

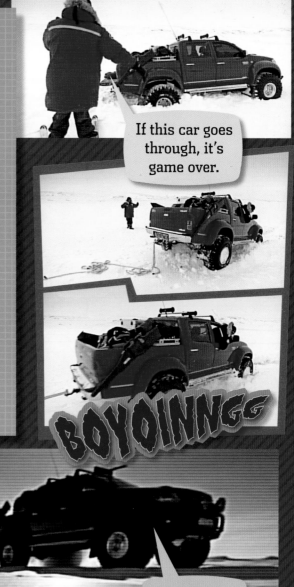

If this car goes through, it's game over.

BOYOINNGG

We can't **not** go near the coast.

It's **blue:** I'm looking at the ocean.

James has a hammer at the ready – if the car falls through the ice, they'll have to smash the windows to get out.

Luckily the ice eventually thickens – but they set up camp knowing there's another challenge ahead in the morning. Jeremy is worried. James cheers him up with food.

If we go in here, we're dead, aren't we? I mean **dead.**

Tomorrow, we hit the **boulder field.**

Quail's egg?

We're likely to be down to two miles a **day.**

Pâté de foie gras?

I think we should leave fairly early.

What would those salmon eggs go **really well** with?

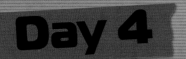

Richard and Matty are covering a lot of ground, but Richard admits he is completely exhausted: at one point, for no other reason, he'd burst into tears on the sledge. Then his tears froze inside his goggles, so he couldn't see where he was going.

The dogs only need a couple of hours' sleep – then they're ready to go again. But they're a bit argumentative.

They're under way, but they're still on Bathurst Island.

So then I had something to cry **about.**

Don't touch him, because he's **scared.** He'll bite **anybody.**

Time for Jeremy and James to get up.

Jeremy's MP3 player and camera have packed up from the cold, so for entertainment he's forced to drive off while James is having a toilet break.

The fun stops when they hit the boulder field – a jumble of blocks of ice the size of houses. They can't drive straight through this and they can't drive around it. Luckily they're 90 miles in front of Richard.

Where's my **tea**, Clarkson?

Very unfunny. Idiot!

Look at it – look at **that!**

Richard has to get off the sledge and push as they encounter a steep hillside.

Jeremy and James have a choice: chop their way through ice boulders, or dig themselves through the 15ft snow drifts between them.

The boulder field is a complete maze. The lads waste time finding routes, which end up just being dead ends.

UFF

Each time we spin the wheels, we sink a little bit more.

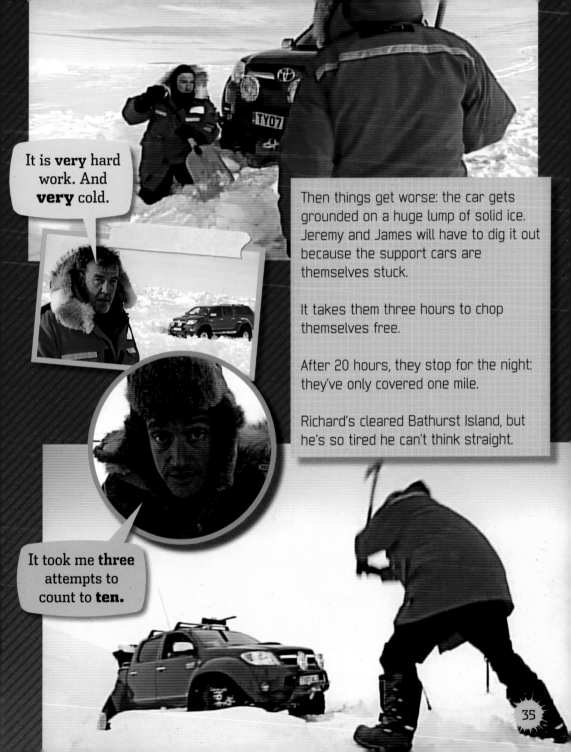

It is **very** hard work. And **very** cold.

Then things get worse: the car gets grounded on a huge lump of solid ice. Jeremy and James will have to dig it out because the support cars are themselves stuck.

It takes them three hours to chop themselves free.

After 20 hours, they stop for the night: they've only covered one mile.

Richard's cleared Bathurst Island, but he's so tired he can't think straight.

It took me **three** attempts to count to **ten.**

Day 5...ish

We're going to be in here **forever.**

After only two hours' sleep, Jeremy and James get to survey what lies ahead. More ice boulders, all the way to the horizon.

They spend the next eight hours going... nowhere.

Richard, for once, is in good spirits as they leave Bathurst Island and head up the fjord. Matty unleashes a secret weapon: a kite. She uses it to pull her along on skis, saving weight on the sledge.

Now we are making progress!

On one of the flatter stretches of the boulder field, Jeremy puts his foot down – until a hidden block of ice rips the extra fuel tank off the bottom of the car. The impact also tears a tyre off its rim and damages the propshaft.

The crash also bent a shock absorber. They've got a spare, but replacing it and the tyre takes time. They also have to pump fuel from the damaged tank into the standard fuel tank. Time ticks away...

It smells **remarkably** like it might be leaking.

BA-DOOM

Sometimes, James, you have to move **fast.**

Sometimes, Jeremy, you have to move **slowly.**

Team Dog is now at the boulder field. James blames Jeremy for the delay.

Jeremy and James get back on their way – but they're both exhausted and Jeremy is soon falling asleep at the wheel.

I am **so unspeakably outraged** with you.

I am **dying!**

You **can't** build a tent by **shouting.**

They have no choice: they have to put the tent up again. It's -42°C. They row again – looks like Sir Ranulph was right about the whole hatred thing.

The dogs are also fighting. Matty has to let fly with a stick, to let them know she's the boss. But they're making good progress through the boulder field.

The Final Push

VRMM VRUMM

James, this bolt is **stuck** to my lips!

Jeremy and James are stuck again. James breaks out the chainsaw to cut through the ice. They also use ramps to bridge the clefts between boulders.

While assembling the ramps, Jeremy makes the mistake of holding a nut between his lips – it freezes to them. Sadly for James, it fails to shut him up. Jeremy's lips are restored to full flapping order with help from some hot coffee.

One of the ramps collapses. They're stuck again!

Richard and Matty are catching up.

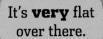
It's **very** flat over there.

We've made it! It's **flat**! It's so **smooth!**

James and Jeremy are finally clear of the boulder field. Their average speed through it: 1mph.

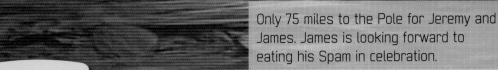

Only 75 miles to the Pole for Jeremy and James. James is looking forward to eating his Spam in celebration.

What if I ate your **Spam?**

You're **not** eating my Spam.

Jeremy and James decide that now victory is certain, they can risk another night of camping. Well, 90 minutes of sleep, at least.

Richard and Matty know they can't afford to stop.

The next 'morning', Jeremy, tired of James' sinuses, decides to shoot the tin of Spam in revenge.

Job done.

I spy with my little eye, something beginning with... S.

Snow?

Yes.

Jeremy and James pass the time with a game of I Spy.

Then they encounter something very surprising: a plane. Specifically, the wreck of an old US Air Force C-47, which crashed here in 1949 (all passengers and crew survived).

Imagine surviving that plane crash and then finding yourself here.

That's a bad deal.

Richard and Matty, after 15 hours on the go, are forced to stop. Richard is now so tired, he can't even speak.

Now only 10 miles from journey's end, Jeremy and James have to stop, too: it's another boulder field. It takes them three hours to cover one mile.

Finally free – and desperately low on fuel – Jeremy goes for it.

Um...

You're going to **bust** it.

I'm **not.**

VRRRAAAAAHHH

The Winner

It's **here!**
Come on!

Ready for it...
ready... **Yes!**

"I will not be beaten by a dog," Jeremy declares: and as it turns out, he's right. After a bit of manoeuvring, he and James arrive at the otherwise featureless stretch of ice that their satnav unit tells them is the Magnetic North Pole (or at least, where it used to be). They've won! And they are the first people ever to drive here.

They phone Richard – who falls off the sledge even before he's heard the news.

◎ Destination
Lat.   :N 78° 35' 7"
Long.   :W 104° 11' 9"

W   N

E

◎ Current position
Lat.   :N 78° 35' 7"
Long.   :W 104° 11' 9"

ooOff

You've done it?

We've **done** it. We're here.

Bad luck.

Sadly, Richard is so far behind, it's not even worth him trying to press on to the Pole. Sadder still, James May actually tries to eat the Spam that Jeremy shot earlier.

Oh...

So What Have We Learnt?

"I set out to prove that polar exploration could be easy," says Jeremy, "but it isn't. It's brutal and savage."

Yet, thanks to their amazingly capable vehicle (and OK, a support crew), two unfit, middle-aged men made it to the Pole.

Glossary

4x4

A four-wheeled vehicle where the engine drives all its wheels, which is why 4x4s are also sometimes called four-wheel-drives (or 4WDs for short).

The Arctic

The region around the North Pole. It's usually defined as the region above the Arctic Circle, which is at latitude 66.56 degrees north.

The Arctic Circle

An imaginary line around the Earth: if you live north of it, then on at least one day a year the sun won't set – it will stay above the horizon even at midnight. The further north from the Arctic Circle you live, the more days of continuous sunlight you get. And if you live at the North Pole, the sun won't set for six months. Unfortunately, for every day of 24-hour sunlight in summer, you'll also have one day in winter when the sun doesn't rise. Pretty grim.

Banjo

Small, guitar-like stringed instrument which originated in Africa. Absolutely no use at all in the Arctic.

Birmingham

Large, low-lying city in the West Midlands. Basically, a really bad place to be born if you want to be a skier.

burning coal, driving cars and (in Jeremy Clarkson's case) talking. Global warming is why polar ice is melting, sea levels are rising and Scottish people are getting suntans. Tiny changes in Earth's temperature (it's risen only about 0.75°C in the past 100 years) have a massive knock-on effect on climate and life on Earth. Some people, however, deny it is happening. These people are idiots.

GPS

A gadget that reads signals beamed down from satellites orbiting Earth and works out your exact position on the planet to within a couple of metres. The letters stands for 'Global Positioning System'. A GPS unit is at the heart of the satellite navigation system (satnav for short) you've probably got one on your car's dashboard (you know, the one with the really annoying voice that the driver is always shouting at).

Body clock

Your body's built-in system that tells you you're tired at night and should sleep, or refreshed in the morning and should therefore get up. It packs up completely in the Arctic, and also during term time.

Fjord

A long, narrow inlet from the sea, usually with steep cliffs either side.

Global Warming

The increase in the average temperature of Earth, mostly caused by an increase of carbon dioxide gas in the atmosphere. Which is mostly caused by humans

It possibly comes from *marche*, the French for 'walk'. Also, apparently, what your brain will turn into if you watch too much TV, according to your mum.

Pâté de foie gras

A meat paste made from the liver of a force-fed goose. Strange but true. Tasty but deeply upsetting to vegetarians.

Sea ice

Ice formed when sea water freezes. Because salt changes the freezing point of water, sea ice doesn't form until the sea temperature drops to around -1.8°C.

Latitude

Imagine you're standing at the centre of Earth (and haven't melted – it's a toasty 3600°C down there). The equator is straight ahead of you, on the level, at 0 degrees latitude. The North Pole is directly overhead – at a 90-degree angle. Which means its latitude is, yes, 90 degrees north. The latitude of any place on Earth is just the angle you'd have to tilt your head at to look at it. So, Paris, for instance, is at 48.8 degrees north while Edinburgh is at 55.9 degrees north.

Mush!

What you traditionally shout at huskies to encourage them to pull your sledge.